The Anguish of Loss

For the Love of Justin

Julie Fritsch
with
Sherokee Ilse

Acknowledgements

The tragedy of my son, Justin's death opened many hearts and doors. I wish to thank the people of whom there are so many, for their loving support and their willingness to offer me encouragement and guidance. A few of these people are first and most importantly Sherokee Ilse, who planted the seed for the book, Lynne DeSpelder, who lightened the load, cleared the path and opened doors, Sue and Jack Gunn, who supported me in all ways, Charlie Smith who fired my fragile sculptures, Laura Grinder who advised and encouraged me, HAND of Santa Cruz, Stanford University and Pat Verdugo.

Above all, my deepest and heartfelt thanks to my loving and supportive husband, Doug, my wonderfully special son, Tosh, my parents for guiding and loving me, and my husband's parents for their quiet patience. I could not have endured without all their love.

J. Fritsch

This book was only a dream that could never have been nurtured to reality without the work and encouragement of many including and especially, Julie Fritsch, a loving mother who, through her work, has carved a lasting tribute to her son, Justin.

Some of the many others I want to appreciate and thank are: Bruce Moulton, Tim Nelson, Susan Erling, Dave Fritz, Judith Benkendorf, Sr., Jane Marie Lamb, Bob Wasiluk, Aldo Palimeri and my special loving family.

Each one played a vital role which added to the richness and quality of this project.

S. Ilse

Photography by: Paul Schraub
Cover and graphic design by: deRuyter Nelson Publications, Inc., Bob Wasiluk, artist

Library of Congress Catalog Card Number 88-92505
ISBN Number 0-9609456-5-2

Printed in the United States, 1988, 1992
Distributed in the United States and Canada simultaneously.

For additional copies write to:
  Wintergreen Press
  3630 Eileen Street
  Maple Plain, MN 55359
  (612) 476-1303

© Copyright 1988 by Julie Fritsch. Second edition 1992.

All rights reserved. No part of this book may be reproduced or transmitted in any form or by an means, electronic or mechanical, including photocopying, recording, or copying by any information storage and retreival system without the written permission of the publisher, except where permitted by law.

Dedication

In memory of my beloved son, Justin Tyson Fritsch, from whom this gift has come.

To all who experience the anguish of loss.

I dedicate this book to all who have loved and suffered. May you feel freer to express your love, emotions and anguish over your loss as you attempt to survive the crisis. My hope is that through sharing my sorrow and grief you, too, will be able to express what is inside of you. May you find comfort in knowing you are not alone and may you find hope in believing you will survive. Someday, may there be light and love and laughter of a different kind in your life.

This book is also dedicated to those who seek to enter into the experience so they may understand and better support those who are suffering, no matter their loss.

Introduction

Sherokee Ilse
Author, *Empty Arms*

When a loved one dies, or tragedy strikes, when the unexpected happens we are overcome with pain and sorrow. The emotions that follow are so intense and personal that it's easy to feel we are the only one experiencing such heartache.

The Anguish of Loss is a heart wrenching account of that pain and loneliness. Through Julie's sculptures, we share her struggle as we each find validation and reminders that we are not alone. Today, such encouragement to feel and express our grief is not fully accepted in our society. Yet, it is the very thing that we each need to do as a part of the healing process.

Our souls do sing the same song, our hearts pulse with a similar beat, and our minds and bodies ache with emptiness after a loss. However, through it all, we are each unique and will experience our bereavement in a manner that is truly our own.

Whether your child has died, your partner, parent, sibling or a dear friend, whether you have experienced a miscarriage, infertility, have lost your job, your pet, your health or a special dream, you will find validation and support within this poignant work.

You need not fear that the intensity and hard grief will be there forever. Although it does last longer than most people hope, more than just a few weeks or months, eventually it will lessen. In the future there will be days when it may be difficult to recall the depth of pain you once felt.

I can attest to this from personal experience. Three of my five pregnancies have ended in loss. I was surrounded with and engulfed by so much sorrow and emotion that I could hardly think clearly. I actively grieved over my losses and after about six difficult months I felt the intensity begin to lessen. I started to have more good days than bad.

In the process of learning to live through this experience, I authored the book *Empty Arms* and co-authored *Miscarriage: A Shattered Dream*. In addition, I helped to found the Pregnancy and Infant Loss Center. I speak nationally on this subject and have authored many booklets and articles. This work was of great benefit to me as I grieved and changed my life's course.

Still, throughout the years since these losses, I have felt some pain and sadness, yet the joys and importance of the good memories now outweigh the bad.

When I first laid eyes on Julie's sculptures at a conference in California six years after my son Brennan's death, I was moved to tears. It surprised me, since I felt most of my tears had been shed and I was unprepared for the fierce emotion that was drawn from my body and soul. Those tears were cleansing for me. It was another opportunity to be with my children, to be with myself, to let go and feel. I was not afraid of the intensity because I knew it was short term and a continuing part of a lifelong process.

I noticed that everyone who walked by the sculpture display was drawn closer to examine them. As I watched, each person began wiping their eyes, reaching for a tissue. It was evident they were deeply moved.

There was something powerful and magnificent about Julie's work. I felt she needed to share it with others who had experienced such tragedies and with those who had not.

During a quiet moment, I thanked her for her gift and for providing another medium to reach out to those who have felt the anguish of loss. I asked if she had noted the response of those who walked by. Then I urged her to consider presenting the pictures of the sculptures in a book. A year later she contacted me to ask if I would consider publishing the pictures in a book. I could only answer, "Yes, of course!"

Creating and birthing a book is a long and arduous experience, but I believe the effort will be meaningful. I hope this book will reach out and serve many purposes such as offering validation for the human condition of loving, suffering, losing, hoping and living again. It reaches all walks of life and touches a basic human chord.

These sculptures and their corresponding emotions may become a measurement or a guide of where you have been and how you are doing. They should also serve as a reminder that the grief and anguish will not last forever. You will be able to survive this experience and you will have other good things in your life. The memory of this difficult time will likely become that; a memory. As hard as it is to believe, you can learn to live again and survive. Maybe you will even grow from the process.

This is a mother's journey, a story shared from her perspective. Although a father's grief might be similar in some respects, it is not specifically dealt with in this book. The intention is not to undervalue men's feelings, but to recognize that *The Anguish of Loss* is from a woman's perspective.

What a lovely gift this book is to share with others. It can teach them about the pain and suffering. Hopefully it will invite their compassion and support.

The Anguish of Loss is also a special contribution of art and culture that will serve as a marker of the significance of childbearing loss in the 1980's. The stonelike sculptures have roots in mythology and cultures of long ago, resulting from past generations who shared their pain, suffering and healing. I have no doubt this work will also stand the test of time and future generations will be able to relate and understand.

I humbly and compassionately share this beautiful work with you in hopes that it helps in some special way.

Sheroker Olse

SHEROKEE ILSE worked with Julie to help create and nourish the development of this book. As the mother of two living children and three babies who died, Sherokee has used her personal experience to reach out and help others in similar situations.

Sherokee is the author of *Empty Arms: Coping with Miscarriage, Stillbirth and Infant Death* and co-author with Linda Hammer Burns of the book *Miscarriage: A Shattered Dream.* She founded the Pregnancy and Infant Loss Center, a non-profit service organization, is a national speaker and consultant on this subject and has authored many articles, pamphlets and booklets for bereaved families and their care providers.

A former teacher, Sherokee has a degree in psychology and sociology from Hamline University, St. Paul, MN. She currently balances family time with her personal and professional commitment to perinatal bereavement.

Introduction

Julie Fritsch

Presented in this book are visual expressions of my grief, sorrow and emotions after what has been the greatest loss in my life, the death of my son, Justin.

These sculptures evolved spontaneously out of a personal need to express my deep feelings of pain. They were created over the course of a year as I worked through the long journey of grief.

I found that after the creation of a few sculptures, I felt relief as each emotion appeared in clay where I could hold it, caress it and form it into a complete statement of what I was feeling. By adding prose, each became more complete.

Through encouragment of friends, the idea of sharing my journey and sculptures to help others through their pain, seemed to put a new light on their existence. Their message seemed to unfold so many hidden and suppressed feelings in those who viewed them, that I felt even more confident I must share them with those in need. Midway through the tunnel of grief and suffering it is so reassuring to realize you are not alone and that there are others who do understand.

I share Justin's tribute with you and I invite you to enter into *The Anguish of Loss* as a soulmate of many others who, too, have traveled this dark and lonely road.

So, render yourself able to express what is inside. Do not be afraid. Then seek support and encouragement from others who will listen and understand.

Julie Fritsch

JULIE FRITSCH is the mother of Justin and her only living son, Tosh, age 11. She and her husband, Doug live in the Santa Cruz area of California where she works and displays in her favorite art medium, sculpture. This book is a series which evolved out of her grief for her second son Justin who was born and died on March 26, 1986. Her grief was compounded by an earlier ectopic pregnancy loss followed by six years of infertility.

Justin was a long awaited and loved child. When he died unexpectedly of an unusual cord accident during the labor process Julie, Doug and Tosh were devastated.

Julie found working through her loss by sculpting in clay to be a tremendous way for her to release her feelings. These rough, raw pieces became a vehicle for her to help herself and others. It has become a special tribute to Justin.

Julie majored in art and found early on that she preferred working in clay. For the past ten years she has specialized in clay sculptures as a way to express herself. She has sold many of her works and continues to create new pieces always finding opportunities to display and share her work.

Stay Within

Don't venture out.
Not yet.
This is to be our only time
to love and be together.
We are still one.

If only I had known
this was our time,
our only time.

Precious Moments

Our precious moments
have come to pass.
They were too few, too few.
I hold you now,
but for only moments.
I waited for such moments
for so long.

My arms, they ache,
a lonesome ache.
For my precious moments
were, oh, so few.

I Say Hello,
But Sadly I Say Goodbye

I say hello, but sadly goodbye,
as I hold you in my arms.
You, whom I have known,
deep within my heart.
You are so real to me.
For moments, yet for all eternity.

Silently I Scream

Silently I scream.
I cannot be heard
except in my very soul.

Holding tighter
each moment that passes,
knowing if I hold on much longer
I will never be able to let go.

I screamed inside with disbelief
as they took you away.
My last chance to touch,
to hold, and to be
with a love that was special
and only known
for too short a time.

Yet known forever.

Sharing The Grief

Hear us crying,
we are in such pain.
Together we must comfort,
and be comforted
by the loving touch, the warmth
and the sadness we share.

In sharing the grief
and the pain
we are still alone,
with our thoughts,
our dreams, our love.

Yet, we are together.

Mother's Milk

My body knows not
that you are gone.

My breasts fill.
My heart aches.
My moans replace
all other sounds.
You are not in your rightful place.
My painful breasts
are only a reminder now,
of what was supposed to be.

But is not.

Sibling Grief

Sibling grief
is so complex
and so sad.
A dream collapses;
pain and confusion take its place.

What can I do
to take your pain
away, my son?
You are not to blame,
you are so innocent,
yet I dare not protect you.
Instead I shall include you.

Silence and pain
they are us.

The Anguish of Loss

The anguish of loss
is overpowering and vast.
I feel as if I'm
paralyzed and lost.
Not of this world.
I'm captured in my body,
not knowing whether
I can be anymore.

Collapsing

Collapsing
from the weight of emotions
I cannot control.

Drained of any ability to cope
or carry on.

I collapse now,
and feel myself overcome
by absolute grief.

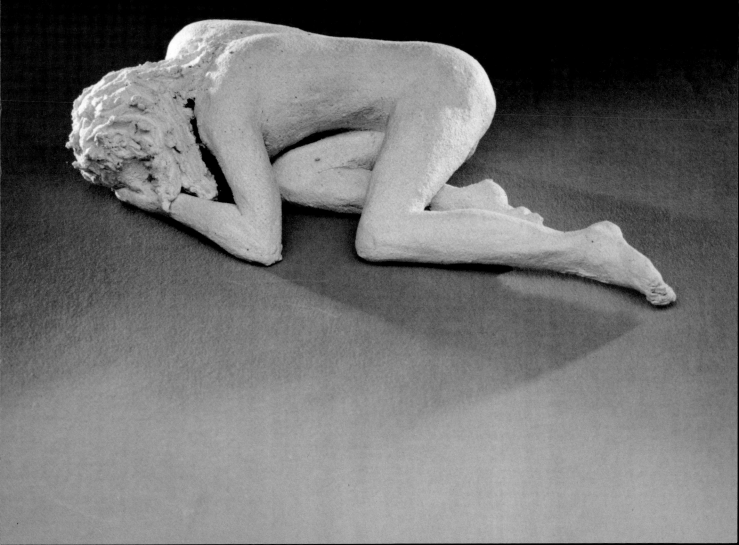

Why?

Why
I ask,
must this be?
Why must this be?

To endure this pain
is to ask for answers.
Why must this be!

Does God know why?
Will He enlighten me?
Will He strengthen my faith,
my beliefs so I can endure?
Will I ever know the answer?

Why!

Trying To Maintain

Trying to maintain,
to keep alive.
Left to go on alone,
despite my desires.

This pain
seems to absorb
my senses.
I feel as if I'm crawling
just to keep myself alive.

Forgive My Tears, My Love

Forgive my tears, my love,
for we alone must share
the sorrow of our hearts.

Born from a perfect soul,
we created together.
Sharing a love and a future
that we alone have lost.

Blanketed In Grief

Together
we are
at a loss for words.

Only our touch
upon each other
is of comfort.

We try to face
each day,
returning each night
to comfort ourselves
and each other,
surrounded by,
a blanket of grief.

Exhaustion

Exhaustion.
It now engulfs me
in a sea of endless tears.
An aching heart,
tired and swollen eyes,
a heavy chest
all weighted down
by pure emptiness.

Emptiness and exhaustion,
I experience more than not.

To Be, Just To Be

It does not end.
How could it end?
I am so full of grief,
learning to live again.

I must endure.
I must survive.
So tired and so full of grief.

I can endure.
I can survive.
To be, just to be, so full of grief.

I will endure!
I will survive!

A Painful Rage

Anger comes silently.
I am overcome by a painful rage,
confusion and feelings
of failure.

Dare I feel such anger?
Such rage?
It screams from within,
needing to get out.

Feeling a loss of control,
my silence and patience
erupt in rage.

Is this me?
Are these my feelings?
Is this my fault?

Must I submit to the rage
in order to be
at peace with myself?

A Quiet Moment

Sharing our needs,
during a quiet moment.

Our lost dreams,
our sadness,
our shattered hopes,
our future.

We are changed,
we are different,
but we are together
in our new selves.
For now,
we share a quiet moment.

My Broken Heart, My Aching Soul

This pain I feel
is like the sea.

The breaking of my heart
like the crashing of the waves.

The aching of my soul
like the ebb of the tide.

My tears are hidden by them both
like the sand
that is covered by the sea.

My broken heart, my aching soul.

Once Again

I begin to live again, slowly,
almost against my wishes.

Yet, once again,
I struggle, then collapse.
Pain and sorrow
once again.

But this time
I don't struggle
as long.
The energy to live
returns sooner.

I struggle
to prepare
for both the calmness
and the sorrow
which are now
part of me.

Forever

We embrace
our understanding of this,
which has been sorrowful,
painful and powerful.

Forever we will hold
in our hearts
that special part of us
that is our son.

Together we will share
and remember,
forever.

Your hand, My Hand

Your hand, my hand.
Your touch, my touch.
Though apart,
we are
forever one.

Additional Loss Resources Available from Wintergreen Press

Empty Arms: Coping with miscarriage, stillbirth and infant death, Sherokee Ilse, 1990

This very unique and special book reaches out to all who have been touched by infant death in a most compassionate manner. Through her own experiences the author offers guidance and comforting support to bereaved families. Over 150,000 in print.

$7.50, plus postage   Substantial bulk rate available.

Miscarriage: A Shattered Dream, Sherokee Ilse and Linda Hammer Burns, 1985.

Miscarriage offers a compelling and insightful perspective on a loss that is quite frequent and most misunderstood. Those who have suffered a miscarriage will find in this book comprehensive medical information, emotional support and helpful coping suggestions. Given by many caring professionals to their patients.

$7.50, plus postage   Substantial bulk rate available.

The Anguish of Loss Slide Show, Julie Fritsch, 1987.

Julie offers slides of her sculptures, in addition to the book. They are powerful and quite useful as a teaching tool to allow people to 'experience' the intensity of loss.

$170, plus postage   Available from Wintergreen Press or Julie Fritsch

Wintergreen Press
3630 Eileen Street
Maple Plain, MN 55359
612-476-1303

Other Helpful Books

A Child Dies: A Portrait of Family Grief, Joan Arnold, Aspen System Corporation, 1983.

Coping With Sudden Infant Death Syndrome, John DeFrain, Lexington Books, 1982.

Don't Take My Grief Away From Me, Doug Manning, Insight Books, 1979.

Empty Arms: Coping with Miscarriage, Stillbirth and Infant Death, Sherokee Ilse, Wintergreen Press, 1982.

How Do We Tell The Children, A Parents' Guide to Helping Children Understand and Cope When Someone Dies, Dan Schaefer and Christine Lyons, Newmarket Press, 1986.

How To Go On Living After the Loss of A Child, Larry Peppers and Ron Knapp, Peachtree Press, 1985.

I Know Just How You Feel...avoiding the cliches of grief, Erin Linn, Publisher's Mark, 1986.

Infertility: A Guide to Childless Couples, Barbara Eck Menning, Prentice Hall, 1977.

Grieving: How to live after the loss of a love, Therese Rando, Research Press, 1988.

Living Through Mourning, Finding Comfort and Hope When a Loved One Has Died, Harriet Sarnoff Schiff, Viking Penguin, Inc, 1986.

Living When a Loved One Has Died, Earl Grollman, Beacon Press, 1977.

Miscarriage: A Shattered Dream, Sherokee Ilse and Linda Hammer Burns, Wintergreen Press, 1985.

Parental Loss of a Child, Therese Rando, Research Press, 1987.

Parting is not Goodbye, Kelly Osmont and Marilyn McFarlane, Nobility Press, 1986.

Stillborn, The Invisible Death, John DeFrain, Lexington Books, 1986.

The Bereaved Parent, Harriet Sarnoff Schiff, Crown Publishing, 1977.

The Wedded Unmother, Kaye Halverson, Augsburg Publishing, 1980.

When Bad Things Happen to Good People, Rabbi Harold Kushner, Schoeken Books, 1981.

When Pregnancy Fails, Barbara Borg and Judith Lasker, Beacon Press, 1981.

Resources

Although there are many books, booklets, audio-visuals and organizations specifically on the subject of miscarriage, infant loss, child loss and bereavement, below are listed but a few that could be a starting place to explore other resources.

Please note that none of these organizations have a 24-hour hotline. Most operate during regular office hours.

The Pregnancy and Infant Loss Center
1421 E. Wayzata Blvd.
Wayzata, MN 55391
612-473-9372
Offers literature, newsletter, national support group information, parent outreach program, and professional training on miscarriage, stillbirth and infant death.

SIDS Alliance
10500 Little Patuxent Parkway
Suite 420
Columbia, MD 21044
800-221-7437
Offers information and referrals to medical, counseling and parent support programs; newsletter; and funds medical research.

SHARE: Pregnancy and Infant Loss Support, Inc.
National Office
St. Joseph's Health Center
300 First Capitol Drive
St. Charles, MO 63301
314-947-5000
Offers assistance to new and ongoing support groups, newsletter, national support group information and special assistance to families and care providers after miscarriage, stillbirth and infant death.

American Association of Suicidology
2459 S. Ash
Denver, CO 80222
303-692-0985
Offers information and education on suicide prevention, as well as state referrals to suicide crisis lines and survivors support groups.

RESOLVE, Inc.
PO Box 474
Belmont, MA 02178
617-643-2424
Offers literature, newsletter, support and referrals to local and state resources on infertility.

The Compassionate Friends
National Headquarters
PO Box 3696
Oak Brook, IL 60522-3696
708-990-0010
A self-help organization of bereaved parents helping each other after their child's death (any age). Many state and local chapters.

Parents of Murdered Children, Inc.
100 E. 8th Street, #B-41
Cincinnati, OH 45237
513-721-5683
Offer information to families about the criminal justice system, the grieving process and referrals to local resources.

M.A.D.D.
511 E. John Carpenter Freeway
Irving, TX 75062
800-438-MADD
Mothers Against Drunk Driving offers assistance to victims through emotional and legal support, information and education.

Bereavement Magazine
PO Box 674
Carmel, IN 46032-2334
317-846-9429
A magazine of hope and healing. All types of death are addressed. Offers referral lists of hundreds of support groups and organizations throughout the U.S. and Canada.

AARP Widowed Persons Services
601 E. St. NW
Washington, D.C. 20049
202-434-2260
Offers education, information and referrals to local and state support groups and individuals.